A Liturgical Catechism

A Liturgical Catechism

QUESTIONS & ANSWERS ABOUT LUTHERAN WORSHIP & DOCTRINE

Daniel V. Biles

With Illustrations by Jeffery Neal Larson

ALPB Books

Delhi, New York

A Liturgical Catechism

Edition following the order of Holy Communion in the *Lutheran Book of Worship* (1978)

The American Lutheran Publicity Bureau wishes to acknowledge and thank Frederick J. Schumacher for bringing this work to the board and championing it, Gregory P. Fryer for his editorial assistance, Jeffery Neal Larson (www.commonrenderings.com) for the illustrations, and Dorothy Zelenko for her proofreading of the text, typesetting and production.

Paul Robert Sauer
Executive Director

The texts for the order of Holy Communion in the chart of the liturgy found on pages 15-20 are taken from *Lutheran Book of Worship* © 1978 Lutheran Church in America, The American Lutheran Church, The Evangelical Lutheran Church in Canada, and the Lutheran Church—Missouri Synod.

English translations of the Apostles' Creed, the Lord's Prayer, the preface dialog, the canticle texts "Glory to God in the highest," "Holy, holy, holy Lord," and "Lamb of God" © 1988 English Language Liturgical Consultation (ELLC). www.englishtexts.org. Used by permission.

American Lutheran Publicity Bureau
P.O. Box 327
Delhi, New York 13753

ISBN 1-892921-31-6

Daniel V. Biles, *Liturgical Catechism: Questions & Answers about Lutheran Worship & Doctrine* (LBW Edition)
Delhi, NY: ALPB Books, 2015.

TABLE OF CONTENTS

vi

INTRODUCTION TO THIS CATECHISM

Some years ago I read something like this statement in a book about ministry: "As we worship, so we believe, and as we believe, so we worship." Liturgy and doctrine are the two ways the apostolic teaching of the first followers of Jesus, that is, the Scriptures, have come down to us (Acts 2.42). Liturgy is in fact prayed doctrine, Christian teaching in the form of prayer.

In the history of the Church, the way we worship and the doctrines the Church developed to summarize and express her faith developed simultaneously. The process has always been mutually reinforcing: as we worship, so we believe, and as we believe, so we worship.

This catechism is based on this principle that as we worship, so we believe, and as we believe, so we worship. It uses the classic liturgy of the Western Church as the setting to explain the basic teachings of the Christian faith and help believers grow in their knowledge of the Church, its teachings, and its practices.

"Catechesis" comes from a Greek word, "to echo back." Early Christian instruction for new believers took the form of questions put before students, to which they were to give the proper answer. This catechism is laid out in this style: each part of the liturgy is used to provide instruction about a topic of Christian teaching, using a question-and-answer format. For some parts, there are written exercises to help students see the interrelationship of Scripture, Christian teaching, and how we worship.

Traditional catechesis centered on the Apostles' (or baptismal) Creed, the Ten Commandments, and the Lord's Prayer. That is, it taught what we are to believe (Creed), how we are to live (Commandments) and how we are to pray (Lord's Prayer). Martin Luther's reform of the Catechism added two more topics: How we become Christians (Baptism) and how we nurture faith (Holy Communion). This catechism treats all of these topics and more, though not in the same order of catechesis such as we see in Luther's catechisms: Commandments, Creed, Lord's Prayer, Baptism, Communion. Indeed, in this catechism the Ten Commandments are treated last of all, as part of the dismissal at the end of the liturgy, under the theme of how we serve God in the world.

It is my hope that laypersons and pastors will find this small book an easy-to-use means of learning the basics of Christian faith and practice.

Pr. Dan Biles
St. Paul Lutheran Church, Spring Grove, PA
www.stpaulchurchsg.org
Lent, 2015

ACKNOWLEDGEMENTS

I am thankful to the ALPB for the publication of this book. Specifically, I thank two colleagues who welcomed this idea and shepherded it from reception to publication: Pastors Gregory Fryer and Fred Schumacher.

This book arose out of a desire to provide a means of catechizing people in the Christian faith that would be reinforced by the worship the Church does each Sunday. "As we worship, so we believe, and as we believe, so we worship" has been the operating principle. So, I thank the congregations I have served in my years in ministry – Good Shepherd, Cincinnati (internship); St. Mark's, Clifton Heights, PA; Bendersville Lutheran Parish, PA; and St. Paul, Spring Grove, PA – for providing me the continual challenge of teaching the faith.

The idea for the format of this book came from reading the catechism in the Episcopal *Book of Common Prayer* (Seabury Press, 1979, pp. 844-862). Specific citations from this catechism are noted as "BCP." Of course, Martin Luther's *Small Catechism* (SC) is used extensively, either directly or in its underlying theology, throughout, along with the Augsburg Confession (AC). The section about "the principles of Christian worship" on pages 11-12 was adapted from an ALPB tract called *How Lutherans Worship* published in 1978. The order of liturgy is from the 1978 *Lutheran Book of Worship* (LBW); the *Manual on the Liturgy* published to accompany the LBW was helpful for general information on the Church's worship.

I also thank those who helped put the book into its final form: Dorothy Zelenko of the ALPB, for her editing and layout work, and Jeffery Larson for his illustrations which he did especially for this book.

When I first wrote this catechism in 2006, I never anticipated it would find its way into print. That it has is thanks to a suggestion by one person: Pr. Sally Gausmann, St. Paul Lutheran Church, Trinity Road, West York, PA. So, thank-you, Sally.

Pr. Dan Biles

4

PREFACE, Part 1: BECAUSE WE ARE BAPTIZED

Q: Why do Christians worship?

A: Christians gather for worship because we have been baptized into Jesus Christ. We see this pattern from the very beginning of the Church (Acts 2.1-47): When the Holy Spirit came upon the disciples, they began preaching the Gospel of Jesus (2.1-36). In response, people asked how they should respond to the Gospel. The answer was repentance and Baptism (2.38). Following Baptism, the first Christians gathered for worship: prayer, listening to the apostolic teaching, Holy Communion (2.42), singing praise to God (2.46-47).

In short, worship is the most natural thing Christians do. It is the unique activity of the Church; no other organization on earth has this privilege and responsibility.

The word "worship" comes from an Anglo-Saxon word, *weorthscipe*, meaning to ascribe worth to or show respect to someone or something. Christians worship God because He is worthy of our respect, our honor, our praise and thanksgiving. Worship is a duty we owe to our fellow believers and to God. For a Christian, not to worship is a denial of who one is.

Q: What is Baptism?

A: Baptism is the means by which people become Christians. It is a sacrament of initiation into the Christian faith.

Q: Why do we baptize?

A: Because Jesus commanded us to baptize. In Matthew 28.16-20, Jesus' final instructions to His followers are to go to all the world and make new followers of Jesus. We are to teach the faith, urge people to follow Jesus, and baptize "in the Name of the Father, the Son, and the Holy Spirit."

Q: What is Christian teaching about Baptism?

A: The Church's teaching about Baptism is summarized in our worship book (LBW, p.121):

In Holy Baptism our gracious heavenly Father liberates us from sin and death by joining us to the death and resurrection of our Lord Jesus. We are born children of a fallen humanity; in the waters of Baptism we are reborn children of God and inheritors of eternal life. Through water and the Spirit we are made members of the Church, the Body of Christ. As we live with Christ and His people, we grow in faith, love, and obedience to the will of God.

a. Baptism Means Freedom: Through Baptism God liberates us from the two greatest forces which afflict us in life, guilt and fear. We feel guilt for the sins we have done or the opportunities to do good we did not take in life. We are anxious about the future, because we are aware of our mortality. Through forgiveness God frees us from guilt over the past; by His promise of life eternal God gives us faith and hope to face the future. (Romans 6.3-5, 11-14; Acts 2.37-39; I Peter 3.20-21)

b. Baptism Means New Birth: From our natural birth we are unable to have true fear and love of God or faith in Him (AC-2). By our own efforts we cannot free ourselves from this condition. Freedom from sin can only come by an act of God. This happens in Baptism. Jesus calls it "being born again by water and the Spirit." Paul in his letter to Titus calls it "a washing of rebirth and renewal by the Holy Spirit." Baptism is being born again: God attaches our life to His, turning us from our rebellion against God to faith in Him and walking in His ways. (Romans 3.9-12; John 3.1-6; Titus 3.4-8)

c. Baptism Means Union With Christ Through His Church: Baptism unites us with Christ by joining us to His Body, the Church, in the power of the Holy Spirit. This community of faith began when God called Abraham and promised him land, descendants, and a mission (Genesis 12.1-3). This community of faith will last until the end of time, when we will join all creation in the praise of God (Revelation 4). In this one, holy, catholic, and apostolic Church we share in the life of God. (I Corinthians 12.13, 27; Galatians 3.26-29)

d. Baptism Means a New Way of Life: Baptism begins a new way of life. The whole of life after Baptism until our resurrection to eternal life is living in the power and promise of God in Baptism.

There is always the danger that we can fall away from what God has made us in Baptism. Life in this world is a continual struggle with sin, death, and evil. Thus, Martin Luther in the *Small Catechism* teaches that every day we need to repent and return to our Baptism, receiving again God's forgiveness, and renewing our intent to walk in righteousness. This is the daily use of Baptism: daily conversion to Christ.

Baptismal faith needs to be nurtured. We grow in the strength of our Baptism by daily repentance and forgiveness, the life of prayer and study of the Scriptures, and most importantly by common worship with other believers. Through these practices we grow into the full maturity of faith (Ephesians 4.15) that God intends for us. (Romans 6.1-11; 12.1-3; Galatians 5.1, 16-25; Ephesians 4.1-6).

Q: Some churches teach that we cannot baptize infants. Is this true?

A: There is no clear word of Jesus in Scripture either commanding or forbidding infant baptism. Therefore, it is a matter of responsible Church decision.

From its beginnings, the Church has practiced infant baptism, for two reasons. One is that Baptism is fundamentally God's work, not ours. Baptism is what God does to us, not what we do for God.

Second, since Baptism is initiation into the Church and the Christian way of life, it can begin at any time. From infancy we learn what it means to belong to our human families; from whatever age we are baptized we learn what it means to belong to God's family. What is important is that Christian parents and godparents and congregations provide for adequate and full nurture of faith in children through programs of worship, education, and service.

Q: What is "Believers' Baptism"?

A: "Believers' Baptism" first developed in the 16th century and is a different understanding of Baptism from the historic teaching of the Church. Believers' baptism holds that one has to make a clear, conscious decision and commitment to Jesus and thus must be old enough to understand this. One is baptized to affirm that one has made this commitment and because Jesus commanded baptism.

The Church from its beginnings taught and practiced a *sacramental* Baptism. That is, Baptism is a means of God's grace. The focus is on what God does to us, not our decision.

The differences can be summarized by these two different lines of thought, based on Mark 16.16: "Whoever believes and is baptized shall be saved."

Believers' Baptism:
1. The Bible says that whoever believes and is baptized shall be saved.
2. I have made a decision for Jesus and have been baptized.
3. Therefore, I will be saved.

Sacramental Baptism:
1. I have been baptized in the Name of the Father, the Son, and the Holy Spirit.
2. God does not lie; His Word is certain and can be trusted.
3. Therefore, I will be saved.

In either case, the Baptism is valid, because it is done "in the Name of the Father, Son, and Holy Spirit," and God's Word makes Baptism valid. The difference is one of emphasis. Both those who practice Believers' Baptism and those who practice Sacramental Baptism believe that we are saved by God, not by our own merits, not even by the good deed of being baptized. But Believers' Baptism puts more emphasis on our experience and decision while Sacramental Baptism stresses God's Word and our trust in His promise.

Q: Some say that only Baptism by immersion is true. Is this so?

A: The teaching that we must be immersed to be truly baptized is based on the teaching that we must baptize in exactly the same way Jesus was baptized. This has not been the historic teaching or practice of the Church, though many baptisms in the early Church were by immersion. The earliest manual of instruction for Baptism, *The Didache*, (2nd Century) shows the Church allowed for a variety of ways of doing Baptism. Baptism is true because of God's Word in Baptism, not because of the way it is done.

PREFACE, Part 2: FUNDAMENTALS OF CHRISTIAN WORSHIP

Q: What is Christian worship?

A: Christian worship is the gathering of Christians to praise and adore our God, to give thanks for His blessings, to hear what the Lord is speaking to us in His Word, to offer our prayers, and to receive God's grace in the Sacrament of Holy Communion.

The Psalmist (Psalm 29.2) invites Christians to "worship the Lord in the beauty of His holiness." That is, Christians should gather to worship the Lord in a way that is beautiful, in a way that refreshes, restores, and inspires our spirits and lifts us beyond our everyday, mundane lives to the presence of God.

Q: What are the principles of Christian worship?

A: Christians worship our God in a wide variety of ways, using different rituals, liturgies, and styles of music reflecting different ethnic groups and cultures. Even so, there are certain principles that are common to Christian worship in its fullest expression:

a. Christian worship follows a common order of service developed and adopted by the Church over the centuries. This order of service revolves around two foci: the "Service of the Word," focusing on hearing God's Word, and the "Service of Holy Communion," which focuses on celebrating the risen Lord Jesus' presence and receiving God's grace in the Lord's Supper.

b. Christian worship is biblical. The roots of our worship go back to the synagogue worship that we see in the Bible (Luke 4.16-21) and the life of the early Church (Acts 2.43-47). Much of the language we use in our worship service is taken directly from the Bible.

c. Christian worship treasures the blessings of our worship heritage. We take care to conserve the hymns, prayers, rituals, and other means of devotion the saints who have gone before us have passed on to our generation. It is our responsibility to conserve and pass on this heritage to the next generation.

d. Christian worship uses the arts, such as music, to glorify God and instruct His people.

e. Christian worship uses the contemporary language of the people to praise and pray to God.

f. Christian worship is liturgical. Liturgy means "a public work of the people." Christian worship is not a spectator sport, in which the congregation watches what the worship leaders do. It is not a show performed by a few people for the entertainment of others. All persons participate in the worship of God through prayer, singing hymns, listening to God's Word, making responses, carrying out rituals, etc. Pastors and laypersons have different roles in worship.

Q: What is "ritual"?

A: Rituals are patterns of actions repeated regularly that symbolize and express the meaning of what we are doing in worship. Rituals are aids to "pay attention to God": they focus attention on what we are doing; they remind us of who we are and express the meaning of our worship.

Christian worship is rich in ritual actions. We stand to praise God and pray to Him. We sit to hear God speak to us. We make the sign of the cross to remind ourselves of our Baptism and Jesus' death for us. Vestments set apart various persons for specific tasks in the service. We use songs and words Christians have used for centuries, which makes us mindful that we belong to a community of faith that has gone before us and to which we will belong for all eternity.

Q: How did our liturgy develop?

A: Christian worship is based on the synagogue worship of Judaism, from which the Christian Church developed. Synagogue worship has these elements, which we see in Luke 4.16-21: Singing of hymns, prayer, reading Scripture, teaching based on the Scripture (sermon). Early Christian worship added to this basic structure one more element, Holy Communion, which celebrates the presence of the risen Lord Jesus with us (I Corinthians 11.23-26).

Q: Is our liturgy biblical?

A: Almost all of our liturgy is drawn from the Bible; some of the words of our liturgy are exact quotes from the Bible. Do the exercise on page 33 to learn how the Bible is used in our worship. Match each Bible verse with the way it is used in our liturgy.

THE LITURGY
Lutheran Book of Worship

	Preparation for Worship
Invocation	P: In the Name of the Father, and of the (+) Son, and of the Holy Spirit. C: Amen.
Confession and Forgiveness	P: Almighty God, to whom all hearts are open, all desires known, and from whom no secrets are hid: Cleanse the thoughts of our hearts by the inspiration of your Holy Spirit, that we may perfectly love you and worthily magnify your holy name, through Jesus Christ our Lord. C: Amen P: If we say we have no sin, we deceive ourselves and the truth is not in us. But if we confess our sins, God who is faithful and just will forgive our sins and cleanse us from all unrighteousness. Most merciful God: C: We confess that we are in bondage to sin and cannot free ourselves. We have sinned against you in thought, word, and deed, by what we have done and by what we have left undone. We have not loved you with our whole heart; we have not loved our neighbors as ourselves. For the sake of your Son, Jesus Christ, have mercy on us. Forgive us, renew us, and lead us, so that we may delight in your will and walk in your ways, to the glory of your holy name. Amen P: Almighty God, in his mercy, has given his Son to die for us and, for his sake, forgives us all our sins. As a called and ordained minister of the Church of Christ and by his authority, I therefore declare to you the entire forgiveness of all your sins, in the name of the Father, and of the (+) Son, and of the Holy Spirit. C: Amen

Service of the Word

Entrance Hymn	
Apostolic Greeting	P: The grace of our Lord Jesus Christ, the love of God, and the communion of the Holy Spirit be with you all. C: And also with you.
Kyrie	P: In peace, let us pray to the Lord. C: Lord, have mercy. P: For the peace from above, and for our salvation, let us pray to the Lord: C: Lord, have mercy. P: For the peace of the whole world, for the well-being of the Church of God, and for the unity of all, let us pray to the Lord: C: Lord, have mercy. P: For this holy house, and for all who offer here their worship and praise, let us pray to the Lord: C: Lord, have mercy. P: Help, save, comfort, and defend us, gracious Lord. C: Amen
Hymn of Praise	P: Glory to God in the highest, and peace to his people on earth. C: Lord God, heavenly king, almighty God and Father: We worship you, we give you thanks, we praise you for your glory. Lord Jesus Christ, only Son of the Father, Lord God, Lamb of God, You take away the sin of the world; have mercy on us. You are seated at the right hand of the Father; receive our prayer. For you alone are the Holy One, you alone are the Lord, you alone are the Most High, Jesus Christ, with the Holy Spirit, in the glory of God the Father. Amen
Prayer of the Day	P: The Lord be with you. C: And also with you. P: Let us pray. . . . (The Prayer of the Day is said.) C: Amen

16

First Lesson	A reading from the Old Testament.
Psalm	A psalm from the Book of Psalms (hymns) is sung or said.
Second Lesson	A reading from the New Testament letters.
Verse	C: Alleluia. Lord, to whom shall we go? You have the words of eternal life. Alleluia. Alleluia.
The Holy Gospel	A reading from one of the Gospels: Matthew, Mark, Luke, or John, with the acclamations before ("Glory to you, O Lord.") and after ("Praise to you, O Christ.")
The Sermon	The Pastor preaches God's Word for today.
The Sermon Hymn	
The Creed (Apostles' or Nicene)	C: I believe in God the Father almighty, creator of heaven and earth. I believe in Jesus Christ, his only Son, our Lord. He was conceived by the power of the Holy Spirit and born of the Virgin Mary. He suffered under Pontius Pilate, was crucified, died, and was buried. He descended into hell. On the third day he rose again. He ascended into heaven, and is seated at the right hand of the Father. He will come again to judge the living and the dead. I believe in the Holy Spirit, the holy catholic Church, the communion of saints, the forgiveness of sins, the resurrection of the body, and the life everlasting. Amen
The Prayers of the Church and Passing of the Peace	P: The peace of the Lord be with you always. C: And also with you.

Service of Holy Communion

The Offering and Offertory	The offering is collected and brought forward, along with the bread and wine for Communion, while a hymn is sung.
Preface	P: The Lord be with you. C: And also with you. P: Lift up your hearts. C: We lift them to the Lord. P: Let us give thanks to the Lord our God. C: It is right to give him thanks and praise.
Proper Preface	P: It is indeed right and salutary that we should give thanks and praise to you, O Lord, Almighty God and Father.... therefore with angels and archangels and all the company of heaven, we praise your name and join their unending hymn:
Sanctus	C: Holy, holy, holy, Lord, God of power and might: Heaven and earth are full of your glory. Hosanna. Hosanna. Hosanna in the highest. Blessed is he who comes in the name of the Lord. Hosanna in the highest.
Prayer of Thanksgiving	P: Holy God, mighty Lord, gracious Father: Endless is your mercy and eternal your reign. You have filled all creation with light and life; heaven and earth are full of your glory. Through Abraham you promised to bless all nations. You rescued Israel, your chosen people. Through the prophets you renewed your promise; and, at this end of all the ages, you sent your Son, who in words and deeds proclaimed your kingdom and was obedient to your will, even to giving his life. In the night in which he was betrayed, our Lord Jesus took bread, gave thanks, broke it, and gave it to his disciples, saying: Take and eat; this is my body given for you. Do this for the remembrance of me. Again, after supper, he took the cup, gave thanks, and gave it for all to drink, saying: This cup is the new covenant in my blood, shed for you and for all people for the forgiveness of sin. Do this for the remembrance of me. For as often as we eat of this bread and drink of this cup, we proclaim the Lord's death until he comes.

	C: Christ has died. Christ is risen. Christ will come again.
	P: Therefore, gracious Father, with this bread and cup we remember the life our Lord offered for us. And, believing the witness of his resurrection, we await his coming in power to share with us the great and promised feast.
	C: Amen. Come, Lord Jesus.
	P: Send now, we pray, your Holy Spirit, the spirit of our Lord and of his resurrection, that we who receive the Lord's body and blood may live to the praise of your glory and receive our inheritance with all your saints in light.
	C: Amen. Come, Holy Spirit.
	P: Join our prayers with those of your servants of every time and place, and unite them with the ceaseless petitions of our great high priest, until he comes as victorious Lord of all.
	C: Through him, with him, in him, in the unity of the Holy Spirit, all honor and glory is yours, almighty Father, now and forever. Amen
Lord's Prayer	C: Our Father in heaven, hallowed be your name, your kingdom come, your will be done, on earth as in heaven. Give us today our daily bread. Forgive us our sins as we forgive those who sin against us. Save us from the time of trial and deliver us from evil. For the kingdom, the power, and the glory are yours, now and forever. Amen
Agnus Dei	C: Lamb of God, you take away the sin of the world; have mercy on us. Lamb of God, you take away the sin of the world; have mercy on us. Lamb of God you take away the sin of the world; grant us peace.
The Distribution	The congregation comes forward to receive the Sacrament, hearing the Word of God: "The body of Christ, given for you" and "The blood of Christ, shed for you."

Post-Communion Canticle	P: The body and blood of our Lord Jesus Christ strengthen you and keep you in his grace. C: Amen Thank the Lord and sing his praise; tell everyone what he has done. Let all who seek the Lord rejoice and proudly bear his name. He recalls his promises and leads his people forth in joy with shouts of thanksgiving. Alleluia. Alleluia.
Post-Communion Prayer	P: We give you thanks, almighty God, that you have refreshed us through the healing power of this gift of life; and we pray that in your mercy you would strengthen us, through this gift, in faith toward you and in fervent love toward one another; for the sake of Jesus Christ our Lord. C: Amen
Benediction	P: The Lord bless you and keep you. The Lord make his face shine on you and be gracious to you. The Lord look upon you with favor and (+) give you peace. C: Amen

The Sending

Dismissal	P: Go in peace. Serve the Lord. C: Thanks be to God.
Final Hymn	

PREPARATION FOR WORSHIP

Invocation
Confession

Q: What is the purpose of the Invocation?

A: The Invocation (p. 15) states the nature and purpose of our worship. We gather for worship at the command and the invitation of our God. The purpose of our coming together is to worship the Lord our God. Gathering in the Lord's Name means we represent to the world the God we worship, the God who is Father, Son and Holy Spirit.

On Sundays when the Confession and Absolution is not used, we use the Apostolic Greeting (p. 16) to greet each other at the start of the service.

Q: Where does God command us to worship Him?

A: The command to worship the Lord our God is given in the Ten Commandments:

I am the Lord your God: You shall have no other Gods before me.

You shall not make for yourself a graven image, or any likeness of anything that is in heaven above or in the earth beneath, or that is in the water under the earth; you shall not bow down to them or serve them . . .

You shall not take the Name of the Lord your God in vain. . . .

Honor the Sabbath Day, to keep it holy.

Q: What are these commandments?

A: These commandments explain our duty to God: to believe and trust in Him, to put nothing in the place of God, to show God respect in our words and deeds, and to set aside regular times for worship, prayer, and the study of God's Word (BCP, p. 847).

Q: Who or what is God?

A: Our god is that to which we look for the source of all good and as our refuge in every time of need (SC, Part I, Commandment 1). The First Commandment states that we are to fear, love, and trust in the Lord our God alone (SC, Part I, Commandment 1).

Q: Where do we learn that the Name of God is "Father, Son, and Holy Spirit"?

A: Jesus tells us in Matthew 28.19 that we are to baptize people "in the Name of the Father, Son, and Holy Spirit."

Q: Why is the phrase "Lord God" or "the Lord our God" sometimes used in the Bible?

A: In the Old Testament, the Name of God in Hebrew is YAHWEH. However, on the basis of the Commandment not to misuse the Name of God, the Jews would not say the Name YAHWEH. Instead, they substituted the title "LORD" (Hebrew, Adonai).

PREPARATION FOR WORSHIP

Invocation
Confession

Q: Why do we do the rite of Confession and Absolution (p. 15) before worship?

A: We prepare for worship by asking God to make us worthy to worship Him, so that we may stand in God's holy place "with clean hands and a pure heart" (Psalm 24.3-4).

Q: What is Confession and Absolution?

A: Confession and Absolution is a rite in which we admit (confess) our sins before God and hear from the Pastor the assurance that God forgives our sins (absolution).

Q: What is sin?

A: Sin is seeking our own will instead of God's will (BCP, p. 848). This fundamental or "original" sin is the sin of Adam and Eve (Genesis 3.1-7). All human beings are marked with this first sin of Adam and Eve. That is, all human beings are born without true fear or love of God (AC-2). This Original Sin distorts our relationship with God and His creation, and our relationships with other people. As the Rite of Confession states, we fail to love God with our whole heart and our neighbor as ourselves.

Q: What are sins?

A: Sins are specific wrong or evil deeds that are a result of our fundamental or "Original" sin. In the Rite of Confession they are called the sins of commission ("what we have done") and omission ("what we have left undone").

Q: Why do we need to confess our sins and receive absolution?

A: Because we cannot by our own reason or strength believe in Christ or come to Him (SC, Creed, Article 3). As the confession states, our wills are in bondage to sin. We need God's grace, His Word of forgiveness, to free us from captivity to our sins to live for God and walk in His ways. The Church teaches that we cannot free ourselves by our own efforts or works, but are freely forgiven and justified when we believe that our sins are forgiven for Christ's sake, who by his death and resurrection has achieved forgiveness and justification for us (AC-4, Romans 4.24-25; 5.6-11; II Corinthians 5.19-21).

Q: How do we know we have sinned?

A: We can examine our life in light of the Ten Commandments and see where we have not kept them (SC, Confession). For example: Have I feared, loved, and trusted the Lord God above all else? Have I gladly sought to learn His Word? Have I called on God in praise and thanksgiving, or used His Name for selfish purposes? Have I shown respect to my parents? Have I loved and respected my spouse? Have I harmed my neighbor in any way, by word or deed, or have I failed to help him in all his physical needs?

Q: How do we know that our sins are forgiven?

A: By God's command and promise, given to the Church: Matthew 16.19-20 and John 20.23.

Q: How can the Pastor announce forgiveness of sins?

A: The Pastor does not forgive sins by his own authority or power, but only by the command and authority of God, given by Jesus to the Church, which calls persons to the ministry of Word and Sacrament so that people may come to saving faith in Christ (AC 5).

Q: Why do we not use the Confession and Absolution every Sunday?

A: This rite is not required to be done at every service. When there is no Holy Communion, it is often omitted. In Easter season and Christmas season, the Confession is also sometimes omitted, because these seasons follow penitential seasons in which Confession is used each Sunday. Some churches, though, begin nearly every liturgy with the Brief Order of Confession and Absolution.

SERVICE OF THE WORD

Entrance Hymn
Apostolic Greeting
Kyrie
Hymn of Praise
Prayer of the Day
Scripture Readings
Sermon
Sermon Hymn
Creed (Confession of Faith)
The Prayers of the Church and the Peace

Q: What are the Entrance Hymn, Apostolic Greeting, Kyrie, and Hymn of Praise? (p. 16)

A: These parts of the liturgy are the way we begin our worship service: with song and prayer.

The Entrance Hymn is a song from the Church's great treasury of hymns. It is usually a hymn of praise to start worship.

The Apostolic Greeting comes from II Corinthians 13.14. This verse of scripture became a standard greeting or farewell in the early Church and unto this day. It expresses the essential characteristics of our relationship with God: that through His grace in Christ and His love, we have fellowship (communion) with God through Their Holy Spirit.

The Kyrie is a series of prayers, sung or said. The prayers are for the peace of God, our salvation, the peace of the world, peace in the Church, the worship service at hand, and for God's continuing care. Each prayer ends, "Lord, have mercy." "Lord" in Greek and Latin is Kyrie. Hence the name for this part of the liturgy.

The Hymn of Praise is a song of praise and adoration of the Triune God: We give praise to God the Father through Jesus His Son in the power of Their Holy Spirit. The Hymn of Praise begins with the Christmas announcement of the angels (Luke 2.14): "Glory to God in the highest, and peace to His people on earth." Thus, this part of the liturgy has been called by its Latin name for these words, *Gloria in Excelsis.* In Easter season we usually use another Hymn of Praise, "This is the Feast," celebrating God's victory over sin, evil, and death in the resurrection of our Lord Jesus. This hymn is drawn from verses from the Book of Revelation.

Q: Why do we begin the service this way?

A: As Martin Luther explains the Second Commandment in his *Small Catechism,* we are not to use God's Name for any deceitful, selfish, superstitious, or evil purpose, but instead to call upon the Lord in prayer, praise, and thanksgiving. So, we begin our worship by praising God and praying for His blessing on ourselves and the world.

SERVICE OF THE WORD

Entrance Hymn
Apostolic Greeting
Kyrie
Hymn of Praise
Prayer of the Day
Scripture Readings
Sermon
Sermon Hymn
Creed (Confession of Faith)
The Prayers of the Church and the Peace

Q: What is this?

A: The Prayer of the Day is a short prayer that concludes the beginning of
       the service. It focuses on the theme of this day of the Church year. It is
       introduced by a greeting (p. 16) in which the Pastor and people ask for
       God's presence to be upon each other.

Q: What is the Church year?

A: The Church year (or liturgical year) is a calendar of the Church's
       annual cycle of worship (different from our usual January - December
       year). The whole story in the Bible about God's deeds and the life and
       salvation of His people in the power of the Holy Spirit is told each year,
       but at different times or "seasons" of the Church year we focus on
       different parts of the story.

       First the Church year is divided into two halves, each with particular
       seasons.

       The first half of the Church year tells the story of Jesus' life and has two
       cycles, each with its own seasons. The first is called the Christmas
       cycle. It has three seasons:

Advent: Sometimes called the "Winter Lent," Advent developed as a time of penitence and preparation for the birth of Christ. It originally was six weeks, modeled on the six weeks of Lent, but was shortened to four. In Advent we recall God's promises to Israel of the Messiah. It is a season that emphasizes hope, both through the coming of God to earth in the Christ-child and for when Christ will come again at the end of time.

Christmas: The birth of Jesus became a popular festival in the third Christian century. It celebrates the incarnation of God in His Son, Jesus.

Epiphany: "Epiphany" means "revealing, to make manifest." This season focuses on God made manifest in the ministry of Jesus. It begins on January 6 with the visit of the Wise Men to the infant Jesus, continues the next Sunday with the remembrance of the Baptism of Jesus, and concludes the Sunday before Ash Wednesday with the Transfiguration of Jesus, which marked the shift from His ministry in Galilee to His road to the cross.

The second cycle is the Easter cycle, which centers on the death and resurrection of Jesus. It also has three seasons;

Lent: Lent (from a word meaning "Spring") is a penitential season to prepare us for the celebration of the death and resurrection of Jesus. It focuses on repentance and confession of sin and reflection on our lives in light of the cross of Christ, His suffering and death. Lent begins with Ash Wednesday and continues to the day before Easter: 40 days, not counting Sundays, which are always celebrations of the resurrection.

Holy Week: This is a special part of the forty days of Lent, recalling the events of the last week of Jesus' life and His death. It begins with Palm Sunday, recalling Jesus' entry into Jerusalem before His Last Supper with His disciples on Maundy Thursday, and His death on Good Friday.

Easter: Easter Sunday is the greatest day of the Church year, the Queen of Sundays. The Easter season is a "week of weeks" (seven Sundays), all celebrating the resurrection of our Lord.

The second half of the Church year is the season after Pentecost, which emphasizes the teachings of Jesus and the life of the Church in the power of the Holy Spirit. The season begins with Pentecost Sunday, which tells the story of the giving of the Spirit (Acts 2), continues for about six months and ends with Christ the King Sunday, the last Sunday of the Church year, which affirms Christ as the final judge and ruler of history.

Q: What are festival days?

A: As the name implies, festival or feast days are special days in the liturgical calendar that celebrate or observe an important event, usually in the life of our Lord. There are *principal festival days,* which take precedence over any other observance: Easter, Ascension, Pentecost, Trinity Sunday, Christmas Day, the Epiphany of our Lord. There are *days of special devotion:* Ash Wednesday and the days of Holy Week. *Lesser festivals* remember the apostles and other New Testament people or events (e.g., the Transfiguration). *Commemoration days* celebrate other biblical people or famous saints of the Church.

Q: How did the Church year develop?

A: Early Christians, being Jews, naturally used the existing Jewish festival days. Because of God's saving act in Jesus, they interpreted these in a new light and developed new practices, most importantly for Good Friday and Easter and then Christmas. The liturgical calendar developed over the first thousand years of Christian history into the form we have today.

On the following pages are exercises you may do to learn about how the words of the liturgy are drawn from the Bible and how the Church year is based on the biblical story. (Answers can be found at the end of the book.)

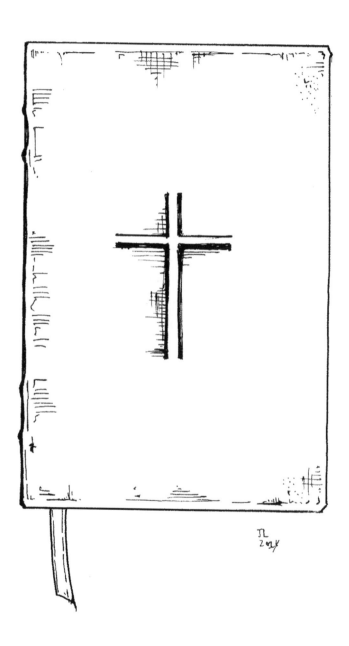

BIBLE STUDY: THE LITURGY

Match the parts of the liturgy on the right with the Bible verses on the left. Some parts, such as the *Sanctus*, have words from more than one scripture verse in them.

_____ I John 1.8-9

_____ II Corinthians 13.14

_____ John 6.68

_____ Isaiah 6.2-3

_____ John 20.19

_____ I Corinthians 11.23-26

_____ Matthew 6.9-13

_____ Numbers 6.24-26

_____ Matthew 17.14-15

_____ Matthew 21.9

_____ Luke 2.14

_____ John 20.23

_____ John 1.29

1. Benediction (Final Blessing, p. 20)

2. Confession of Sins (p. 15)

3. *Agnus Dei* ("Lamb of God," p. 19)

4. Hymn of Praise (p. 16)

5. The Lord's Prayer (p. 19)

6. Prayer of Thanksgiving (p. 18)

7. Apostolic Greeting (Start of Service, p. 16)

8. *Kyrie* ("Lord have mercy," p. 16)

9. *Sanctus* ("Holy, Holy, Holy," p. 18)

10. Passing of the Peace (p. 17)

11. The verse sung between the second lesson and the reading of the Gospel (p. 17)

12. Absolution (Confession and Forgiveness, p. 15)

BIBLE STUDY: THE CHURCH YEAR

Match the Bible verses on the right with the appropriate events of the Church Year on the left.

_____ Christmas: the birth of Jesus (December 25)

_____ The Circumcision of Jesus (January 1)

_____ Epiphany: the visit of the Wise Men (January 6)

_____ The Baptism of Jesus

_____ The Temptation of Jesus (First Sunday in Lent)

_____ The Wedding at Cana: Jesus' first miracle (Second Sunday after the Epiphany)

_____ The Transfiguration of our Lord (Last Sunday in the season of Epiphany)

_____ Palm Sunday: Jesus' entry into Jerusalem

_____ Maundy Thursday: the Lord's Supper

_____ Good Friday: the death of Jesus

_____ Easter: the resurrection of Jesus

_____ The Ascension of our Lord: 40 days after Easter

_____ Pentecost: Giving of the Holy Spirit, 50 days after Easter

_____ All Saints' Day: remembering those who have died in the faith.

_____ Christ the King Sunday: the return of Christ to judge the living and the dead (Last Sunday of the Church Year)

1. Mark 9.2-9

2. I Corinthians 11.23-26

3. Mark 1.4-11

4. Acts 2.1-21

5. Mark 15

6. Luke 2.1-20

7. Matthew 2.1-12

8. I Corinthians 15.20-28

9. Mark 16.1-7

10. Luke 2.21

11. Revelation 7.13-14

12. Mark 11.1-11

13. Acts 1.1-11

14. John 2.1-11

15. Matthew 4.1-11

SERVICE OF THE WORD

Apostolic Greeting
Kyrie
Hymn of Praise
Prayer of the Day
Scripture Readings

>   Old Testament Lesson
>   Psalm
>   New Testament Reading
>   The Holy Gospel

Sermon
Sermon Hymn
Creed (Confession of Faith)
The Prayers of the Church and the Peace

Q: What are the Scripture readings?

A: The Scripture readings are texts from the Bible. They are read so
      that we listen to God as He spoke "in many and various ways to
      His people from of old" (Hebrews 1.1). The readings are chosen
      to match the season of the Church year.

Q: What is the Bible?

A: The Bible (Greek: "Book") is the record of God's Word and deeds
      in the story of His people the Jews and the Church.

Q: How is the Bible the Word of God?

A: We believe that while the Bible was written by human authors,
      God inspired and guided them in their writing (II Timothy 3.16-17),
      and that God through His Holy Spirit continues to speak to us

through the Holy Scriptures to guide the Church and keep us steadfast in Jesus' Word (John 8.31-32; 16.12-13).

Q: What is a lectionary?

A: A lectionary is an assigned series of Scripture readings for the Church year. Our church uses a three-year lectionary which has also been adopted by many other church bodies. Each year uses one of the first three Gospels (Matthew, Mark, or Luke), with readings from John's Gospel used at various points in all three years.

Q: What Scripture texts are used?

A: The First Lesson is usually from the Old Testament, which tells the story of God and His chosen people, the Jews. The books of the Old Testament were probably written down from the years 1000-300 BC, though much of the material in the first five books (called the Pentateuch or Torah) covers the Creation of the world and the years 1600 - 1200 BC.

SERVICE OF THE WORD

Apostolic Greeting
Kyrie
Hymn of Praise
Prayer of the Day
Scripture Readings
Sermon
Sermon Hymn
Creed (Confession of Faith)
The Prayers of the Church and the Peace

Q: What is the Sermon?

A: The Sermon (Latin: *sermonis*, talk) is God's Word spoken to us today through the Pastor. In the Scripture readings we heard God's Word spoken to His people of old; in the Sermon the living God speaks to us today.

Q: Why is the Sermon important?

A: Because by our own efforts we cannot come to Christ or believe in Him as our Savior. But the Holy Spirit calls us through the Gospel and through the Gospel creates faith and keeps us and the whole Church on earth united in the true faith (SC, Creed, Article 3).

Q: Is this belief based on Scripture?

A: Scripture teaches that in order for us to come to saving faith, God instituted the office of ministry; that is, established the preaching of His Word and the administration of the holy sacraments. Through these means the Holy Spirit works faith, when and where He pleases, in those who hear the Gospel (AC 5; Romans 10.14-17; John 20.31; I John 1.1-3). This ministry was established by Jesus Himself (John 20.21-23; Acts 1.8).

Q: How should a Christian listen to a sermon?

A: One should listen to hear in a sermon how God is judging and blessing him or her. That is: What sin does the sermon reveal that I am doing? How does it show that I have fallen short of what God expects of me? How does the sermon proclaim God's blessing to me? How does God forgive me, show His love for me, justify me in spite of my sins? How does the sermon instruct me in living a righteous life, doing what God expects of me (Micah 6.6-8)?

Q: Can any Christian preach?

A: Lutherans teach that no person should preach or administer the sacraments unless they have been specifically called by God through the Church (AC 14). The ministry of the Gospel is not a human creation, but established by God in His Church. Therefore, one is approved and called by the Church to the holy ministry (see the letters of Paul to Timothy and Titus).

SERVICE OF THE WORD

Apostolic Greeting
Kyrie
Hymn of Praise
Prayer of the Day
Scripture Readings
Sermon
Sermon Hymn
Creed (Confession of Faith)
The Prayers of the Church and the Peace

Q: What is the Apostles' Creed?

A: The Apostles' Creed (p. 17) is the Church's confession of faith. It is the creed (Latin: *credo:* "I believe") Christians confess at their Baptism. Having heard God's Word in the Sermon, we respond to God's Word by praising God in song and confessing our faith in Him, the faith into which we were baptized.

Q: Is the Creed based on the Bible?

A: All of the Creeds are based on Holy Scripture. Do the exercise at the end of this section to learn how each sentence or phrase in the Creed is based on Scripture.

Q: Are there other creeds the Church confesses?

A: In addition to the Apostles' Creed, the one, holy, catholic and apostolic Church confesses the Nicene and Athanasian Creeds. The Nicene Creed was approved by the whole Church at the Council of Nicea in AD 325 and expanded in AD 381. The Athanasian Creed probably dates from the Fifth or Sixth century and is a teaching creed; it proclaims the nature of the Holy Trinity and the Son of God, Jesus Christ.

Q: What is the Doctrine of the Trinity?

A: The Doctrine of the Trinity is the Christian Doctrine of God. We believe in one God in three persons: Father, Son, and Holy Spirit. Christians worship God the Father through the Son in the power of Their Holy Spirit.

Q: What do we mean by confessing God as Father?

A: We learn that God is the Creator of all things. Therefore, the universe is good (Genesis 1.31, BCP p. 846). It is the creation of a loving God who creates and sustains all things. We are created, male and female, by this same God in His image for a special relationship with Him and to care for God's creation (Genesis 1.26-30, 2.15). Therefore, all human beings have eternal worth before God (Psalm 8). This same God our Father daily provides all we need for life (SC, Creed, Article 1).

Q: What do we mean by confessing God as Jesus Christ, His only Son?

A: We mean that Jesus is the ultimate, complete revelation of God (Colossians 1.15; John 1.18). Jesus shows us the true nature of God: that He is love (I John 4.7-11). For our salvation God became a human being, that through Jesus' death and resurrection he who knew no sin might be made sinful, so that baptized into Christ we who are sinners before God might be made righteous and be reconciled to God (II Corinthians 5.18-21).

Q: What does the Virgin Birth mean?

A: It means that Jesus was born of a woman; thus He is a human being. And, since He was conceived by the Holy Spirit, Jesus is also the Son of God: divine.

Q: What is the importance of Jesus' death and resurrection?

A: It means that God in Christ suffered in every way as we do, without sin, yet was raised to new life. By this God has conquered sin, evil, and death.

Q: What does it mean to say that Jesus sits at the right hand of God?

A: It means that Jesus now reigns as Lord over all the universe (Philippians 2.9-11). This rule is hidden now, but will be revealed at the end of time as the true power that rules the universe.

Q: What do we mean by confessing God as the Holy Spirit?

A: The Holy Spirit is the presence of God the Father and the Son at work in the world and the Church today.

Q: What does the Holy Spirit do?

A: The Holy Spirit leads the Church into and keeps it steadfast in the truth of Christ (John 14.25-26; 16.13-15). Through the ministry of the Gospel the Holy Spirit creates and keeps us united in Christian faith (AC 5; SC Creed, Article 3). Thus, the Holy Spirit creates and sustains the Church (I Corinthians 12.13).

BIBLE STUDY: THE CREED

Match the Bible verses on the right with the correct phrase from the Apostles' Creed on the left.

_____	I believe in God, the Father Almighty,	1. John 1.18
_____	Creator of heaven and earth.	2. Acts 2.1-4
_____	I believe in Jesus Christ, His only Son,	3. Matthew 25.31-46
_____	our Lord.	4. Luke 2.1-7
_____	He was conceived by the Holy Spirit	5. Mark 15.1-20
_____	and born of the Virgin Mary.	6. Ephesians 4.6
_____	He suffered under Pontius Pilate,	7. Acts 2.36
_____	was crucified,	8. Luke 1.26-31
_____	died,	9. Mark 15.21-25
_____	and was buried.	10. Genesis 1.1
_____	He descended into hell.	11. I Peter 3.18-20
_____	On the third day He rose again.	12. Acts 1.6-10
_____	He ascended into heaven,	13. Hebrews 12.2
_____	and is seated at the right hand of the Father.	14. I Corinthians 15.20-28
_____	He will come again to judge the living and the dead.	15. Mark 15.33-37
_____	I believe in the Holy Spirit,	16. I Corinthians 15.3
_____	the holy catholic Church,	17. Matthew 16.18-19
_____	the communion of saints,	18. Mark 15.42-47
_____	the forgiveness of sins,	19. I Corinthians 10.16-17
_____	the resurrection of the body,	20. Mark 16.1-7
_____	and the life everlasting. Amen.	21. John 3.16

SERVICE OF THE WORD

Apostolic Greeting
Kyrie
Hymn of Praise
Prayer of the Day
Scripture Readings
Sermon
Sermon Hymn
Creed (Confession of Faith)
The Prayers of the Church and the Peace

Q: What are the "Prayers of the Church"?

A: Having heard God's Word and confessed our faith, the congregation
      offers prayers for the Church, the world, and all people in need,
      whether Christian or not.

Q: What is prayer?

A: Prayer is listening and speaking to God. It is offering up to God our
      concerns, our thanksgiving, and our praise.

Q: What kinds of prayer are there?

A: There are four principal kinds of prayer. One can best remember them
      with the word, "ACTS":

      A: Adoration or praise of God for Who He is, for His Creation and
            acts of salvation.
            Adoration is simply the enjoyment of God. God as He is
            naturally draws out of us praise.

      C: Confession of our sins.

      T: Thanksgiving for all God's gifts, especially His grace in Christ.

44

S: Supplication, or intercession, in which we pray for our needs and especially the needs of other people, Christian or not, and concerns in the world.

Q: What is the "Peace"?

A: The Passing of the Peace (p. 17) is the bridge between the Service of the Word and the Service of Holy Communion. Up to this point in the service we have prepared for worship through confessing our sins and receiving God's Word of forgiveness. We have praised God and brought our prayers before Him. We have listened to God in scripture and sermon, confessed our faith in song and creed, and offered our prayers to God for ourselves, the Church, and all people throughout the world. Now at this point in the service we exchange a personal greeting of God's peace with our fellow believers and prepare to come to the Table of the Lord united in God's peace. The greeting of peace recalls Jesus' greeting to his followers when he appeared to them after the resurrection. His greeting of peace dispelled their fears, lifted their faith, and gave them courage to serve Him (John 20.19-21).

Q: What should we do in the Passing of the Peace?

A: Simply greet those around you with these or similar words, "The peace of God (or the Lord) be with you."

SERVICE OF HOLY COMMUNION

The Offering and Offertory
The Holy Communion
      Preface and Proper Preface
      The Sanctus
      Prayer of Thanksgiving
      Lord's Prayer
      Agnus Dei
      Distribution
      Post-Communion Canticle
      Post-Communion Prayer
      Blessing

Q: What is the Offering?

A: Offerings of money are an expression of love and gratitude for God's blessings. Along with the gifts of money, bread and wine are presented for use in the Holy Communion. A song (canticle) is sung and a prayer said.

Q: Why should we give an offering to God?

A: The offering prayer expresses what the offering means. We offer to God what He has first given us out of His goodness and love: our lives, our possessions. These are given to honor and give thanks to God and to serve His good purposes on earth. There are several reasons why Christians should do this:

a. To glorify God (Philippians 4.14-20).

b. To follow Jesus' example of giving and service (Philippians 2.5-11). Giving is a Christian lifestyle, as seen in the earliest accounts we have of the Church's life (Acts 2.43-47).

c. To give thanks for God's blessings (Psalm 136). In Romans 1.21, St. Paul identifies *lack of thanksgiving* as a mark of unbelievers.

d. As a sign of trust in God, that we do not seek security in our wealth, but in God's providence (I Timothy 6.17-20).

e. To do their fair share of supporting the work of the Church (II Corinthians 8.1-7).

Q: What is stewardship?

A: This is a term often used for making offerings to the Church, but it has to do with more than just money. Stewardship means to care for something that has been entrusted to us to oversee. In the Bible, a steward is someone who manages someone else's possessions. Christians are stewards of God's possessions, for everything in creation belongs to God (Psalm 24.1). God wants us to take good care of His creation. One way we do this is offering back to God a generous portion of what He has first given to us, as an act of worship, faith, service, and trust (II Corinthians 9.6-15).

Q: What is the Christian way to give?

A: The Scriptures offer practical advice on how to give. In the Old Testament, this was the "law of the tithe," giving 10% of one's income (Leviticus 27.30-32). In the New Testament, St. Paul encourages believers to set aside each week a portion of their weekly income, as they have been blessed, to support the work of God's Church (I Corinthians 16.1-4). There are several basic principles of Christian giving:

a. Giving is disciplined. The practice of making offerings to the Lord curbs our sinful desires to covet what others have, to hoard things for ourselves, to only live to indulge our pleasures.

b. Giving is systematic. Whether weekly, monthly, or by some other schedule, believers work out a system of giving their wealth. One expression of systematic giving is making a pledge each year of what we will give to the Lord.

c. Giving is regular: It is not haphazard, subject to the whims of the moment.

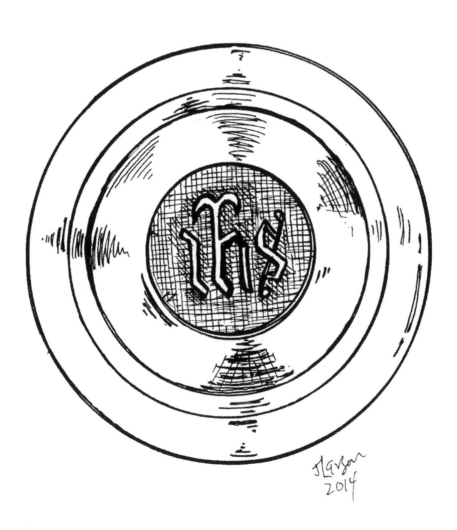

SERVICE OF HOLY COMMUNION

The Offering and Offertory
The Holy Communion
      Preface and Proper Preface
      The Sanctus
      Prayer of Thanksgiving
      Lord's Prayer
      Agnus Dei
      Distribution
      Post-Communion Canticle
      Post-Communion Prayer
      Blessing

Q: What is Holy Communion?

A: Holy Communion is the sacrament commanded by Christ for the continual remembrance of His life, death, and resurrection, until He comes again (BCP, p. 859). In the bread and wine of this sacrament the risen Lord Jesus is present to forgive sins and nurture faith. (SC, Lord's Supper, Questions 1, 3)

Q: What is a sacrament?

A: A sacrament is a visible means and sign of God's grace. Through the visible element(s) of a sacrament God speaks to us and gives His grace to us to strengthen our faith. In a sacrament God attaches His Word to an earthly element to give us a visible demonstration of His grace (e.g., water in Baptism, bread and wine in Holy Communion).

Q: What is grace?

A: Grace is God's favor toward us. By His grace God forgives our sins, assures us of salvation, guides our life, and strengthens our faith.

Q: What sacraments does the Lutheran Church observe?

A: With the whole Church on earth, Lutherans practice Holy Baptism and Holy Communion. Some Lutheran confessional documents regard Private Confession and Absolution as a third sacrament.

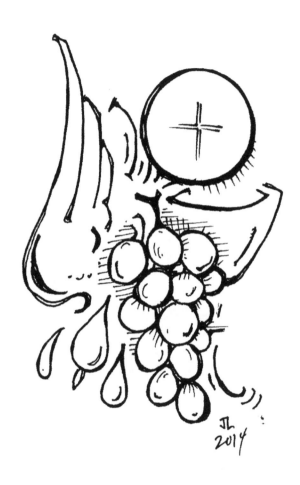

Q: What are other sacraments observed in some churches?

A: The Roman Catholic, Orthodox Church, and Anglican (Episcopal) Church practice the following as sacraments:

Confirmation

Private Confession and Absolution (Penance)

Marriage

Ordination to the Holy Ministry

Extreme Unction (Last Rites)

Q: What are other names for Holy Communion?

A: The Lord's Supper, the Mass, the Great Thanksgiving, Eucharist (Greek: Thanksgiving), and the Sacrament of the Altar are common names for this sacrament.

Q: What blessings does God give us in this sacrament?

A: In this sacrament God forgives our sins, strengthens our faith and unity with Christ, and strengthens us in the hope of salvation. This sacrament is also a visible expression of the unity of all Christians with one another in Christ.

Q: Where does the Bible teach us to observe this sacrament?

A: The command of Jesus to His Church to observe this sacrament is recorded in I Corinthians 11.23-26, Mark 14, Matthew 26, and Luke 22.

Q: How do we receive the benefits of Holy Communion?

A: We receive what God offers us in this sacrament when we believe (trust) in God's Word, "given for you for the forgiveness of sins" as we receive the bread and wine.

Q: How often should the Church celebrate Holy Communion?

A: The command of Christ "Do this in remembrance of me" was understood by the Church at the beginning of its history to mean a weekly Sunday celebration of this sacrament. It is the Lord both Who commands and invites us to His Table, and Who is the gift we receive at His Table.

Q: Explain the parts of the Communion liturgy.

The Preface (p. 18) is three responses, which date from at least the second century of the Church. The Pastor and congregation exchange greetings that the Lord God will be with them in this sacrament. They lift up their hearts in praise and thanks to God for what they are about to receive.

The Proper Preface (p. 18) is a short statement of thanksgiving to God appropriate to the particular season or day of the Church year.

The Sanctus (p. 18) recalls the hymn of heaven (Isaiah 6.1ff and Revelation 4.8) that is continually sung before God, linking it with the coming of Christ to Jerusalem prior to His death and resurrection (Mark 11.10), His coming to us now in the sacrament and His coming again at the end of time.

The Prayer of Thanksgiving (p. 18) recalls God's saving deeds in creation, in the story of His people Israel, and in His Son Jesus. We recall in this prayer the institution of the Lord's Supper as the means of proclaiming Jesus' death and resurrection for us and as our hope of salvation. We pray for the Holy Spirit to make the bread and wine the body and blood of Christ to strengthen our faith. Finally, we pray for God to join our celebration of this sacrament with the life of the whole Christian Church in heaven and on earth and we look forward to when Our Lord Jesus will come again. Therefore, we pray with confidence the prayer our Lord taught us (p. 19).

The Agnus Dei (Lamb of God) (p. 19) is a hymn sung as we begin to receive the sacrament; it recalls John the Baptist's declaration of Jesus in John 1 as "the Lamb of God who takes away the sin of the world."

The Post-Communion Canticle (p. 20) is sung following the Distribution of the sacrament. (A canticle is simply a song, often one where the words are taken from the Bible.) At the close of the Last Supper, "when they had sung a hymn, they went out to the Mount of Olives" (Mark 14.26). Christ has come to us under the forms of bread and wine, and we too respond with song.

The Post-Communion Prayer (p. 20) thanks God for what we have just received. We offer a prayer that the sacrament will have its desired effect in our life: to strengthen our faith, unite us with God and each other, and promote love in the Church and following the example of Christ.

The Benediction (blessing) (p. 20) ends the service; it is the blessing used by God's people since the time of the Exodus from Egypt (Numbers 6.24-26).

THE SENDING

Dismissal

Q: What is the Dismissal?

A: The Dismissal (p. 20) ends the service and directs us to our service to God and others in daily life in the coming week. The Pastor proclaims, "Go in peace, serve the Lord." In the original Latin liturgy, this dismissal was *Missae in pacem,* from which we get the word "Mass." (An interesting oddity is that people say they are "going to Mass," when the word Mass means to "go out.") *Missae* is related to the word "mission" in English, which is what Christians are sent to do in this world.

Q: What does it mean to "Go in peace?"

A: In the worship service we have received and celebrated the peace with God we have through our Lord Jesus Christ (Romans 5.1ff). This peace is the foundation of our life, no matter what else may happen to us in the week to come.

Q: How do we serve the Lord?

A: We serve God by being guided by and doing His commands (Psalm 1; John 15.12-14), by walking in the ways of the Lord (Psalm 119.1-6).

Q: How do we know God's ways?

A: God has revealed His ways in Scripture, especially the Ten Commandments and the "Great Commandments" Jesus taught us.

Q: What are the Ten Commandments?

A: The Ten Commandments were given by God to Israel when God established His covenant with them (Exodus 19 - 20).

Q: What do we learn from the Ten Commandments?

A: We learn from the Ten Commandments how God expects His people to live and act, because we belong to God. In the Ten Commandments we learn our duties to God and to other people (BCP, p. 847).

Q: What is our duty to God?

A: The first three commandments focus on our loyalty to God. We are to fear, love and trust God above all else (SC). We are not to worship any other gods. We are not to misuse God's Name for any evil purpose, but call on God in prayer, praise, and thanksgiving (SC). We are to set aside time each Sunday to worship God and study His Word.

Q: What is our duty to our neighbor?

A: The remaining seven commandments focus on responsibilities in our relationships to other people, beginning with our parents and extending outward. We are to treat our parents with respect. We are not to deliberately harm others, but help them in their physical needs. We are to be faithful in marriage to our spouse. We are not to steal or harm others' property, but help them keep what is theirs. We are to speak kindly and truthfully about others, not falsely or in ways that will harm them. Last, we are to control our desires for other people or things and not seek to gain what is not ours.

Q: What are the Great Commandments?

A: Jesus condensed the entire Ten Commandments into two: to love God with all our heart, soul, and might (Commandments 1-3) and to love our neighbors as ourselves (Commandments 4-10).

Suggested answers to exercises: (Readers may in some cases make different choices that could also be correct.)

Page 33, The Liturgy: 2, 7, 11, 9, 10, 6, 5, 1, 8, 9, 4, 12, 3.

Page 34, The Church Year: 6, 10, 7, 3, 15, 14, 1, 12, 2, 5, 9, 13, 4, 11, 8

Page 43, The Creed: 6, 10, 1, 7, 8, 4, 5, 9, 15, 18, 11, 20, 12, 13, 3, 2, 17, 19, 16, 14, 21

51938576R00037

Made in the USA
Charleston, SC
01 February 2016